50 Spicy Food Recipes for Home

By: Kelly Johnson

Table of Contents

- Spicy Shrimp Tacos
- Spicy Thai Basil Chicken
- Spicy Beef Stir Fry
- Spicy Black Bean Soup
- Spicy Chicken Curry
- Spicy Szechuan Noodles
- Spicy Cajun Jambalaya
- Spicy Sriracha Wings
- Spicy Chipotle Chili
- Spicy Korean BBQ Ribs
- Spicy Buffalo Cauliflower Bites
- Spicy Mango Salsa
- Spicy Garlic Shrimp Pasta
- Spicy Jalapeno Poppers
- Spicy Sichuan Mapo Tofu
- Spicy Cajun Shrimp and Grits
- Spicy Chicken Enchiladas
- Spicy Thai Coconut Soup (Tom Yum)
- Spicy Korean Fried Chicken
- Spicy Salsa Verde
- Spicy Szechuan Eggplant
- Spicy Tandoori Chicken
- Spicy Chipotle Black Bean Tacos
- Spicy Thai Peanut Noodles
- Spicy Cajun Dirty Rice
- Spicy Mango Chicken Curry
- Spicy Korean Kimchi
- Spicy Buffalo Chicken Dip
- Spicy Jalapeno Cornbread
- Spicy Singapore Noodles
- Spicy Sriracha Deviled Eggs
- Spicy Chicken Tortilla Soup
- Spicy Chipotle Hummus
- Spicy Thai Basil Beef
- Spicy Cajun Crab Cakes

- Spicy Szechuan Green Beans
- Spicy Korean Bibimbap
- Spicy Mango Habanero Salsa
- Spicy Buffalo Chicken Sliders
- Spicy Jalapeno Mac and Cheese
- Spicy Thai Green Curry
- Spicy Cajun Chicken Pasta
- Spicy Chipotle Lime Shrimp
- Spicy Korean Bulgogi
- Spicy Szechuan Dan Dan Noodles
- Spicy Mango Chicken Salad
- Spicy Buffalo Cauliflower Pizza
- Spicy Jalapeno Margarita
- Spicy Thai Red Curry
- Spicy Cajun Shrimp Po' Boy

Spicy Shrimp Tacos

Ingredients:

- 1 lb large shrimp, peeled and deveined
- 2 tablespoons olive oil
- 2 cloves garlic, minced
- 1 teaspoon chili powder
- 1/2 teaspoon cumin
- 1/2 teaspoon paprika
- 1/4 teaspoon cayenne pepper (adjust to taste)
- Salt and pepper to taste
- 8 small flour or corn tortillas
- 1 cup shredded cabbage or lettuce
- 1 avocado, sliced
- 1/4 cup diced tomatoes
- 1/4 cup chopped cilantro
- Lime wedges, for serving

Instructions:

1. In a bowl, combine the shrimp with olive oil, minced garlic, chili powder, cumin, paprika, cayenne pepper, salt, and pepper. Toss to coat the shrimp evenly.
2. Heat a skillet over medium-high heat. Add the seasoned shrimp to the skillet and cook for 2-3 minutes on each side until they are pink and cooked through.
3. Warm the tortillas in a separate skillet or in the microwave.
4. To assemble the tacos, place a spoonful of shredded cabbage or lettuce on each tortilla. Top with cooked shrimp, avocado slices, diced tomatoes, and chopped cilantro.
5. Serve the spicy shrimp tacos with lime wedges on the side for squeezing over the tacos.
6. Enjoy your delicious and flavorful spicy shrimp tacos!

Spicy Thai Basil Chicken

Ingredients:

- 1 lb boneless, skinless chicken breasts or thighs, thinly sliced
- 2 tablespoons vegetable oil
- 3 cloves garlic, minced
- 2 Thai bird's eye chilies, thinly sliced (adjust to taste)
- 1 red bell pepper, thinly sliced
- 1 onion, thinly sliced
- 1 cup fresh basil leaves, torn
- 2 tablespoons oyster sauce
- 1 tablespoon soy sauce
- 1 tablespoon fish sauce
- 1 tablespoon brown sugar
- 1/2 teaspoon sesame oil
- Cooked rice, for serving

Instructions:

1. In a bowl, mix together the oyster sauce, soy sauce, fish sauce, brown sugar, and sesame oil. Set aside.
2. Heat the vegetable oil in a large skillet or wok over medium-high heat.
3. Add the minced garlic and sliced Thai chilies to the skillet and stir-fry for about 30 seconds until fragrant.
4. Add the thinly sliced chicken to the skillet and stir-fry for 3-4 minutes until it is cooked through and slightly browned.
5. Push the chicken to one side of the skillet and add the sliced red bell pepper and onion. Stir-fry for an additional 2-3 minutes until the vegetables are tender-crisp.
6. Pour the sauce mixture over the chicken and vegetables in the skillet. Stir well to coat everything evenly.
7. Add the torn basil leaves to the skillet and toss everything together until the basil is wilted.
8. Remove the skillet from heat and serve the spicy Thai basil chicken immediately over cooked rice.
9. Enjoy your flavorful and aromatic spicy Thai basil chicken!

Spicy Beef Stir Fry

Ingredients:

- 1 lb flank steak, thinly sliced against the grain
- 2 tablespoons soy sauce
- 1 tablespoon oyster sauce
- 1 tablespoon hoisin sauce
- 1 tablespoon rice vinegar
- 2 teaspoons cornstarch
- 2 tablespoons vegetable oil
- 3 cloves garlic, minced
- 1 tablespoon fresh ginger, minced
- 1 red bell pepper, thinly sliced
- 1 green bell pepper, thinly sliced
- 1 onion, thinly sliced
- 2 green onions, chopped (for garnish)
- Cooked rice, for serving

For the sauce:

- 1/4 cup beef broth or water
- 2 tablespoons soy sauce
- 1 tablespoon hoisin sauce
- 1 tablespoon sriracha sauce (adjust to taste)
- 1 teaspoon sesame oil

Instructions:

1. In a bowl, whisk together the soy sauce, oyster sauce, hoisin sauce, rice vinegar, and cornstarch. Add the thinly sliced flank steak to the bowl and toss to coat the meat evenly. Let it marinate for about 15-20 minutes.
2. In a separate bowl, mix together the beef broth or water, soy sauce, hoisin sauce, sriracha sauce, and sesame oil to make the sauce. Set aside.
3. Heat 1 tablespoon of vegetable oil in a large skillet or wok over high heat. Add the marinated beef slices and stir-fry for 2-3 minutes until browned. Remove the beef from the skillet and set aside.
4. In the same skillet, heat the remaining tablespoon of vegetable oil. Add the minced garlic and ginger, and stir-fry for about 30 seconds until fragrant.

5. Add the sliced bell peppers and onion to the skillet and stir-fry for 2-3 minutes until they are tender-crisp.
6. Return the cooked beef to the skillet and pour the sauce over the beef and vegetables. Stir well to combine and coat everything evenly.
7. Cook for an additional 1-2 minutes until the sauce thickens slightly and coats the beef and vegetables.
8. Remove the skillet from heat and garnish the spicy beef stir fry with chopped green onions.
9. Serve the spicy beef stir fry immediately over cooked rice.
10. Enjoy your delicious and flavorful spicy beef stir fry!

Spicy Black Bean Soup

Ingredients:

- 2 tablespoons olive oil
- 1 onion, diced
- 2 cloves garlic, minced
- 2 teaspoons ground cumin
- 1 teaspoon chili powder
- 1/2 teaspoon smoked paprika
- 1/4 teaspoon cayenne pepper (adjust to taste)
- 2 (15-ounce) cans black beans, drained and rinsed
- 4 cups vegetable or chicken broth
- 1 (14.5-ounce) can diced tomatoes
- 1 cup frozen corn kernels
- 1 lime, juiced
- Salt and pepper to taste
- Chopped fresh cilantro, for garnish
- Sour cream or Greek yogurt, for serving (optional)
- Sliced avocado, for serving (optional)
- Tortilla chips, for serving (optional)

Instructions:

1. Heat the olive oil in a large pot over medium heat. Add the diced onion and cook for 3-4 minutes until softened.
2. Add the minced garlic, ground cumin, chili powder, smoked paprika, and cayenne pepper to the pot. Stir well and cook for another 1-2 minutes until fragrant.
3. Add the drained and rinsed black beans, vegetable or chicken broth, diced tomatoes (with their juices), and frozen corn kernels to the pot. Stir to combine.
4. Bring the soup to a simmer, then reduce the heat to low. Let it simmer for 15-20 minutes to allow the flavors to meld together.
5. Using an immersion blender or a regular blender, puree about half of the soup until smooth. This helps to thicken the soup while still leaving some texture.
6. Stir in the lime juice and season the soup with salt and pepper to taste.
7. Ladle the spicy black bean soup into bowls and garnish with chopped fresh cilantro.
8. Serve the soup hot, optionally topped with a dollop of sour cream or Greek yogurt, sliced avocado, and tortilla chips on the side.

9. Enjoy your comforting and flavorful spicy black bean soup!

Spicy Chicken Curry

Ingredients:

- 500g chicken breasts, diced
- 2 tablespoons vegetable oil
- 1 onion, finely chopped
- 3 cloves garlic, minced
- 1 tablespoon ginger, minced
- 2 tomatoes, diced
- 1 tablespoon tomato paste
- 1 teaspoon ground turmeric
- 2 teaspoons ground cumin
- 2 teaspoons ground coriander
- 1 teaspoon paprika
- 1/2 teaspoon chili powder (adjust to taste)
- 1 cup coconut milk
- Salt to taste
- Fresh cilantro leaves for garnish

Instructions:

1. Heat the vegetable oil in a large pan over medium heat. Add the chopped onion and cook until softened, about 5 minutes.
2. Add the minced garlic and ginger, and cook for another 2 minutes until fragrant.
3. Add the diced chicken breasts to the pan and cook until they are browned on all sides.
4. Stir in the diced tomatoes, tomato paste, ground turmeric, ground cumin, ground coriander, paprika, and chili powder. Cook for about 5 minutes, stirring occasionally.
5. Pour in the coconut milk and bring the mixture to a simmer. Reduce the heat to low and let the curry simmer gently for about 15-20 minutes, or until the chicken is cooked through and the sauce has thickened.
6. Taste and adjust the seasoning with salt if needed.
7. Serve the spicy chicken curry hot, garnished with fresh cilantro leaves. Enjoy with steamed rice or naan bread.

Feel free to adjust the spice levels and ingredients according to your taste preferences!

Spicy Szechuan Noodles

Ingredients:

- 8 oz (about 225g) dried noodles (such as spaghetti or Chinese egg noodles)
- 2 tablespoons sesame oil
- 2 tablespoons vegetable oil
- 3 cloves garlic, minced
- 2 teaspoons ginger, minced
- 2 tablespoons Szechuan peppercorns, crushed
- 2 tablespoons chili paste or chili oil (adjust to taste for desired spice level)
- 2 tablespoons soy sauce
- 1 tablespoon rice vinegar
- 1 tablespoon brown sugar
- 1 teaspoon Chinese five-spice powder
- 1 cup thinly sliced vegetables (such as bell peppers, carrots, and snap peas)
- 2 green onions, thinly sliced (for garnish)
- Toasted sesame seeds (for garnish)

Instructions:

1. Cook the noodles according to the package instructions until al dente. Drain and rinse under cold water to stop the cooking process. Toss with 1 tablespoon of sesame oil to prevent sticking and set aside.
2. In a large skillet or wok, heat the vegetable oil over medium heat. Add the minced garlic, ginger, and crushed Szechuan peppercorns. Stir-fry for 1-2 minutes until fragrant.
3. Add the chili paste or chili oil to the skillet and stir-fry for another minute.
4. Stir in the soy sauce, rice vinegar, brown sugar, and Chinese five-spice powder. Cook for another minute until the sauce is well combined and slightly thickened.
5. Add the sliced vegetables to the skillet and stir-fry for 2-3 minutes until they are tender-crisp.
6. Add the cooked noodles to the skillet and toss everything together until the noodles are well coated in the spicy sauce and heated through.
7. Remove from heat and drizzle with the remaining tablespoon of sesame oil. Toss to combine.
8. Serve the spicy Szechuan noodles hot, garnished with sliced green onions and toasted sesame seeds.

Enjoy these flavorful and spicy noodles as a satisfying meal! Adjust the level of chili paste or chili oil to suit your taste preferences.

Spicy Cajun Jambalaya

Ingredients:

- 1 tablespoon olive oil
- 1 onion, diced
- 1 bell pepper, diced
- 2 celery stalks, diced
- 3 cloves garlic, minced
- 1 lb (450g) chicken breast, diced
- 1 lb (450g) smoked sausage or andouille sausage, sliced
- 1 can (14.5 oz) diced tomatoes
- 1 cup long-grain white rice
- 2 cups chicken broth
- 2 teaspoons Cajun seasoning
- 1 teaspoon paprika
- 1/2 teaspoon dried thyme
- 1/2 teaspoon dried oregano
- 1/2 teaspoon cayenne pepper (adjust to taste)
- Salt and pepper to taste
- Chopped fresh parsley for garnish

Instructions:

1. Heat the olive oil in a large skillet or Dutch oven over medium heat. Add the diced onion, bell pepper, and celery. Cook, stirring occasionally, until the vegetables are softened, about 5-7 minutes.
2. Add the minced garlic to the skillet and cook for an additional 1-2 minutes until fragrant.
3. Push the vegetables to one side of the skillet and add the diced chicken breast to the other side. Cook until the chicken is browned on all sides, about 5 minutes.
4. Stir in the sliced smoked sausage or andouille sausage, diced tomatoes (with their juices), and rice. Cook for 2-3 minutes, stirring occasionally.
5. Pour in the chicken broth and add the Cajun seasoning, paprika, dried thyme, dried oregano, and cayenne pepper. Stir well to combine.
6. Bring the mixture to a simmer, then reduce the heat to low. Cover and cook for 20-25 minutes, or until the rice is tender and most of the liquid has been absorbed, stirring occasionally.

7. Taste and adjust the seasoning with salt and pepper if needed.
8. Remove from heat and let the jambalaya sit, covered, for 5 minutes to allow the flavors to meld together.
9. Serve the spicy Cajun jambalaya hot, garnished with chopped fresh parsley.

Enjoy this flavorful and comforting dish inspired by the vibrant cuisine of Louisiana!

Adjust the level of cayenne pepper to suit your desired level of spiciness.

Spicy Sriracha Wings

Ingredients:

- 2 lbs (about 900g) chicken wings, split at joints and tips discarded
- 2 tablespoons vegetable oil
- Salt and pepper to taste
- 1/2 cup Sriracha sauce
- 1/4 cup soy sauce
- 2 tablespoons honey
- 2 tablespoons rice vinegar
- 2 cloves garlic, minced
- 1 tablespoon sesame oil
- 1 tablespoon sesame seeds (optional, for garnish)
- Thinly sliced green onions (optional, for garnish)

Instructions:

1. Preheat your oven to 400°F (200°C). Line a baking sheet with aluminum foil and place a wire rack on top.
2. In a large bowl, toss the chicken wings with vegetable oil, salt, and pepper until evenly coated.
3. Arrange the seasoned wings in a single layer on the wire rack. Bake in the preheated oven for 40-45 minutes, flipping halfway through, or until the wings are golden brown and crispy.
4. While the wings are baking, prepare the Sriracha sauce. In a small saucepan, combine Sriracha sauce, soy sauce, honey, rice vinegar, minced garlic, and sesame oil. Cook over medium heat, stirring occasionally, until the sauce thickens slightly, about 5-7 minutes. Remove from heat.
5. Once the wings are cooked, transfer them to a large bowl. Pour the Sriracha sauce over the wings and toss until evenly coated.
6. Optionally, sprinkle the wings with sesame seeds and thinly sliced green onions for garnish.
7. Serve the spicy Sriracha wings hot, and enjoy!

These wings are perfect for game day or any occasion where you want to spice things up a bit! Adjust the amount of Sriracha sauce to your desired level of spiciness.

Spicy Chipotle Chili

Ingredients:

- 1 lb ground beef (or ground turkey for a leaner option)
- 1 onion, diced
- 3 cloves garlic, minced
- 1 red bell pepper, diced
- 1 green bell pepper, diced
- 2 (14.5-ounce) cans diced tomatoes
- 1 (15-ounce) can tomato sauce
- 1 (15-ounce) can kidney beans, drained and rinsed
- 1 (15-ounce) can black beans, drained and rinsed
- 2 chipotle peppers in adobo sauce, minced (adjust to taste)
- 2 tablespoons adobo sauce (from the chipotle pepper can)
- 2 tablespoons chili powder
- 1 teaspoon ground cumin
- 1 teaspoon smoked paprika
- Salt and pepper to taste
- Optional toppings: shredded cheese, sour cream, diced avocado, chopped cilantro, sliced jalapenos

Instructions:

1. In a large pot or Dutch oven, cook the ground beef over medium-high heat until browned and cooked through, breaking it apart with a spoon as it cooks.
2. Add the diced onion, minced garlic, diced red bell pepper, and diced green bell pepper to the pot. Cook for 5-6 minutes, stirring occasionally, until the vegetables are softened.
3. Stir in the diced tomatoes, tomato sauce, kidney beans, black beans, minced chipotle peppers, adobo sauce, chili powder, ground cumin, smoked paprika, salt, and pepper.
4. Bring the chili to a simmer, then reduce the heat to low. Cover and let it simmer for 20-30 minutes, stirring occasionally, to allow the flavors to meld together.
5. Taste the chili and adjust the seasoning if needed, adding more salt and pepper or additional chipotle peppers for extra heat.
6. Serve the spicy chipotle chili hot, garnished with your favorite toppings such as shredded cheese, sour cream, diced avocado, chopped cilantro, and sliced jalapenos.

7. Enjoy your hearty and flavorful spicy chipotle chili!

Spicy Korean BBQ Ribs

Ingredients:

- 2 racks of pork ribs (about 4-5 lbs or 1.8-2.3 kg)
- 1 cup soy sauce
- 1/2 cup brown sugar
- 1/4 cup rice vinegar
- 1/4 cup mirin (Japanese rice wine)
- 1/4 cup sesame oil
- 4 cloves garlic, minced
- 2 tablespoons grated fresh ginger
- 2 tablespoons Korean red pepper paste (gochujang)
- 1 tablespoon Korean red pepper flakes (gochugaru)
- 2 green onions, finely chopped (for garnish)
- Toasted sesame seeds (for garnish)

Instructions:

1. Preheat your oven to 300°F (150°C). Line a large baking dish with aluminum foil.
2. In a bowl, whisk together soy sauce, brown sugar, rice vinegar, mirin, sesame oil, minced garlic, grated ginger, Korean red pepper paste, and Korean red pepper flakes until well combined.
3. Place the racks of ribs in the prepared baking dish, meaty side up. Pour the marinade over the ribs, ensuring they are evenly coated on both sides.
4. Cover the baking dish tightly with aluminum foil and let the ribs marinate in the refrigerator for at least 4 hours, or preferably overnight.
5. Once marinated, remove the ribs from the refrigerator and let them come to room temperature for about 30 minutes.
6. Transfer the baking dish to the preheated oven and bake the ribs, covered with foil, for 2 to 2.5 hours, or until the meat is tender and starts to pull away from the bones.
7. Remove the foil from the baking dish and increase the oven temperature to 425°F (220°C). Brush the ribs with the marinade from the baking dish.
8. Return the ribs to the oven and bake, uncovered, for an additional 15-20 minutes, or until the ribs are caramelized and slightly charred on the edges.
9. Once cooked, remove the ribs from the oven and let them rest for a few minutes. Sprinkle with chopped green onions and toasted sesame seeds for garnish.

10. Serve the spicy Korean BBQ ribs hot and enjoy the delicious flavors!

These ribs are perfect for a backyard barbecue or any gathering where you want to impress with bold and spicy Korean flavors. Adjust the amount of Korean red pepper paste and flakes according to your desired level of spiciness.

Spicy Buffalo Cauliflower Bites

Ingredients:

- 1 head cauliflower, cut into florets
- 1/2 cup all-purpose flour
- 1/2 cup water
- 1 teaspoon garlic powder
- 1/2 teaspoon paprika
- 1/2 teaspoon salt
- 1/4 teaspoon black pepper
- 1/4 cup hot sauce (such as Frank's RedHot)
- 2 tablespoons unsalted butter, melted
- 1 tablespoon honey or maple syrup (optional, for sweetness)
- 1 tablespoon olive oil
- Ranch or blue cheese dressing, for serving
- Celery sticks, for serving

Instructions:

1. Preheat your oven to 450°F (230°C). Line a large baking sheet with parchment paper.
2. In a large bowl, whisk together the all-purpose flour, water, garlic powder, paprika, salt, and black pepper until smooth and well combined.
3. Add the cauliflower florets to the bowl with the batter, and toss until they are evenly coated.
4. Spread the cauliflower florets in a single layer on the prepared baking sheet. Bake in the preheated oven for 20-25 minutes, or until they are golden brown and crispy, flipping halfway through.
5. While the cauliflower is baking, prepare the spicy buffalo sauce. In a small bowl, combine the hot sauce, melted butter, honey or maple syrup (if using), and olive oil. Stir until well combined.
6. Once the cauliflower is done baking, remove it from the oven and transfer it to a large bowl. Pour the spicy buffalo sauce over the cauliflower florets and toss until they are evenly coated.
7. Return the coated cauliflower to the baking sheet and bake for an additional 5-7 minutes, or until the sauce is heated through and the cauliflower is crispy.

8. Serve the spicy buffalo cauliflower bites hot, with ranch or blue cheese dressing for dipping and celery sticks on the side.

These spicy buffalo cauliflower bites are a delicious vegetarian alternative to traditional buffalo wings, perfect for parties or game day snacks! Adjust the amount of hot sauce to your desired level of spiciness.

Spicy Mango Salsa

Ingredients:

- 2 ripe mangoes, peeled, pitted, and diced
- 1 red bell pepper, diced
- 1/2 red onion, finely chopped
- 1 jalapeño pepper, seeded and finely chopped
- 1/4 cup fresh cilantro, chopped
- Juice of 1 lime
- 1 tablespoon honey or maple syrup (optional, for sweetness)
- 1/2 teaspoon ground cumin
- Salt to taste

Instructions:

1. In a large bowl, combine the diced mangoes, red bell pepper, red onion, jalapeño pepper, and chopped cilantro.
2. In a small bowl, whisk together the lime juice, honey or maple syrup (if using), ground cumin, and salt until well combined.
3. Pour the lime dressing over the mango mixture in the large bowl and toss until everything is evenly coated.
4. Taste the salsa and adjust the seasoning, adding more salt or lime juice if needed.
5. Cover the bowl and refrigerate the spicy mango salsa for at least 30 minutes to allow the flavors to meld together.
6. Once chilled, give the salsa a final stir and serve it cold as a topping for grilled fish, chicken, tacos, or tortilla chips.

This spicy mango salsa adds a burst of sweet, tangy, and spicy flavors to any dish, making it perfect for summer gatherings or as a refreshing snack. Adjust the amount of jalapeño pepper to your desired level of spiciness. Enjoy!

Spicy Garlic Shrimp Pasta

Ingredients:

- 8 oz (about 225g) spaghetti or your favorite pasta
- 1 lb (about 450g) large shrimp, peeled and deveined
- 4 cloves garlic, minced
- 1 teaspoon red pepper flakes (adjust to taste)
- 1/4 cup olive oil
- Salt and black pepper to taste
- 1/4 cup chopped fresh parsley
- 2 tablespoons lemon juice
- Grated Parmesan cheese for serving (optional)

Instructions:

1. Cook the pasta according to the package instructions until al dente. Drain and set aside, reserving about 1/2 cup of pasta water.
2. While the pasta is cooking, heat the olive oil in a large skillet over medium heat. Add the minced garlic and red pepper flakes, and cook for about 1-2 minutes, stirring frequently, until the garlic is fragrant and golden brown.
3. Add the shrimp to the skillet and season with salt and black pepper to taste. Cook the shrimp for about 2-3 minutes on each side, or until they are pink and opaque.
4. Once the shrimp are cooked, add the cooked pasta to the skillet along with the chopped parsley and lemon juice. Toss everything together until the pasta is well coated with the garlic-infused oil and the shrimp are evenly distributed.
5. If the pasta seems too dry, add some of the reserved pasta water, a little at a time, until you reach your desired consistency.
6. Taste and adjust the seasoning with salt, pepper, or more red pepper flakes if desired.
7. Serve the spicy garlic shrimp pasta hot, garnished with grated Parmesan cheese if desired.

This spicy garlic shrimp pasta is quick and easy to make, perfect for a weeknight dinner or special occasion. Enjoy the flavorful combination of garlic, red pepper flakes, and succulent shrimp tossed with al dente pasta!

Spicy Jalapeno Poppers

Ingredients:

- 12 fresh jalapeno peppers
- 8 oz (about 225g) cream cheese, softened
- 1 cup shredded cheddar cheese
- 1/2 teaspoon garlic powder
- 1/2 teaspoon onion powder
- 1/2 teaspoon paprika
- Salt and black pepper to taste
- 1 cup breadcrumbs
- 2 eggs, beaten
- Cooking spray or vegetable oil for greasing

Instructions:

1. Preheat your oven to 375°F (190°C). Line a baking sheet with parchment paper and set aside.
2. Cut the jalapeno peppers in half lengthwise and remove the seeds and membranes using a spoon. Be careful to avoid touching your face or eyes while handling the jalapenos.
3. In a mixing bowl, combine the softened cream cheese, shredded cheddar cheese, garlic powder, onion powder, paprika, salt, and black pepper. Mix until well combined.
4. Stuff each jalapeno half with the cream cheese mixture, using a spoon or piping bag to fill them evenly.
5. In one shallow bowl, place the beaten eggs. In another shallow bowl, place the breadcrumbs.
6. Dip each stuffed jalapeno half into the beaten eggs, then coat it thoroughly with breadcrumbs, pressing gently to adhere.
7. Place the breaded jalapeno poppers on the prepared baking sheet in a single layer.
8. Lightly spray or brush the tops of the jalapeno poppers with cooking spray or vegetable oil to help them crisp up.
9. Bake in the preheated oven for 20-25 minutes, or until the jalapeno poppers are golden brown and crispy.
10. Remove from the oven and let them cool slightly before serving.

11. Serve the spicy jalapeno poppers hot as an appetizer or snack.

These spicy jalapeno poppers are sure to be a hit at any party or gathering. Enjoy the creamy and cheesy filling with a kick of heat from the jalapenos! Adjust the level of spiciness by removing or keeping the seeds and membranes of the jalapenos.

Spicy Sichuan Mapo Tofu

Ingredients:

- 1 block (about 14 oz or 400g) firm tofu, cut into small cubes
- 2 tablespoons vegetable oil
- 2 cloves garlic, minced
- 1-inch piece of ginger, minced
- 2 green onions, chopped (white and green parts separated)
- 2 tablespoons Sichuan peppercorns, crushed
- 2 tablespoons doubanjiang (fermented chili bean paste)
- 1 tablespoon chili oil
- 1 tablespoon soy sauce
- 1 teaspoon sugar
- 1 cup chicken or vegetable broth
- 1 tablespoon cornstarch mixed with 2 tablespoons water (slurry)
- Salt to taste
- Chopped cilantro for garnish (optional)

Instructions:

1. Heat the vegetable oil in a wok or large skillet over medium heat. Add the minced garlic, ginger, and white parts of the green onions. Stir-fry for 1-2 minutes until fragrant.
2. Add the crushed Sichuan peppercorns to the wok and continue to stir-fry for another minute.
3. Stir in the doubanjiang (fermented chili bean paste) and chili oil. Cook for 1-2 minutes, stirring constantly.
4. Add the cubed tofu to the wok and gently stir to coat it with the spicy sauce.
5. Pour in the soy sauce, sugar, and chicken or vegetable broth. Bring the mixture to a simmer and let it cook for about 5-7 minutes to allow the flavors to meld together.
6. Carefully add the cornstarch slurry to the wok, stirring continuously until the sauce thickens to your desired consistency.
7. Taste the Mapo Tofu and adjust the seasoning with salt if needed.
8. Garnish with the green parts of the chopped green onions and chopped cilantro (if using).
9. Serve the spicy Sichuan Mapo Tofu hot with steamed rice.

This Spicy Sichuan Mapo Tofu is full of bold and flavorful ingredients, making it a comforting and satisfying dish. Adjust the amount of chili oil and doubanjiang according to your desired level of spiciness. Enjoy!

Spicy Cajun Shrimp and Grits

Ingredients:

For the Shrimp:

- 1 lb (about 450g) large shrimp, peeled and deveined
- 2 tablespoons Cajun seasoning
- 2 tablespoons olive oil
- 2 cloves garlic, minced
- 1 tablespoon lemon juice
- Salt and black pepper to taste

For the Grits:

- 1 cup stone-ground grits
- 4 cups water or chicken broth
- 1 cup shredded cheddar cheese
- 1/4 cup heavy cream or milk
- 2 tablespoons unsalted butter
- Salt and black pepper to taste

For Garnish:

- Chopped green onions
- Chopped fresh parsley

Instructions:

1. Prepare the grits according to the package instructions. In a medium saucepan, bring the water or chicken broth to a boil. Stir in the grits and reduce the heat to low. Cook, stirring occasionally, for about 20-25 minutes or until the grits are thick and creamy. Stir in the shredded cheddar cheese, heavy cream or milk, and butter until well combined. Season with salt and black pepper to taste. Keep warm while you prepare the shrimp.
2. In a bowl, toss the peeled and deveined shrimp with Cajun seasoning, salt, black pepper, minced garlic, and lemon juice until evenly coated.

3. Heat olive oil in a large skillet over medium-high heat. Add the seasoned shrimp to the skillet and cook for 2-3 minutes per side, or until they are pink and opaque. Be careful not to overcook the shrimp.
4. Once the shrimp are cooked, remove them from the skillet and set aside.
5. To serve, spoon the creamy grits onto serving plates or bowls. Top with the cooked Cajun shrimp. Garnish with chopped green onions and fresh parsley.
6. Serve the Spicy Cajun Shrimp and Grits hot and enjoy the delicious flavors!

This Spicy Cajun Shrimp and Grits recipe combines creamy grits with flavorful and spicy shrimp, creating a hearty and satisfying dish that's perfect for any meal of the day.

Adjust the amount of Cajun seasoning according to your desired level of spiciness.

Spicy Chicken Enchiladas

Ingredients:

For the Enchilada Sauce:

- 2 tablespoons vegetable oil
- 2 tablespoons all-purpose flour
- 4 tablespoons chili powder
- 1/2 teaspoon garlic powder
- 1/2 teaspoon onion powder
- 1/2 teaspoon ground cumin
- 1/4 teaspoon cayenne pepper (optional, for extra spice)
- 2 cups chicken or vegetable broth
- 1 can (8 oz) tomato sauce
- Salt and black pepper to taste

For the Filling:

- 2 cups cooked shredded chicken
- 1 cup shredded cheese (such as cheddar or Monterey Jack)
- 1 can (4 oz) diced green chilies
- 1/2 cup chopped fresh cilantro
- 1/2 teaspoon ground cumin
- Salt and black pepper to taste

For the Enchiladas:

- 8-10 flour tortillas (8-inch)
- Prepared enchilada sauce
- Prepared chicken filling
- Additional shredded cheese for topping
- Chopped fresh cilantro for garnish
- Sour cream and sliced jalapeños for serving (optional)

Instructions:

1. Preheat your oven to 375°F (190°C). Grease a 9x13-inch baking dish and set aside.

2. To make the enchilada sauce, heat the vegetable oil in a saucepan over medium heat. Stir in the flour and chili powder, and cook for 1 minute, stirring constantly. Stir in the garlic powder, onion powder, ground cumin, and cayenne pepper (if using). Gradually whisk in the chicken or vegetable broth and tomato sauce. Bring the sauce to a simmer and cook for 10-15 minutes, or until thickened. Season with salt and black pepper to taste.
3. In a mixing bowl, combine the cooked shredded chicken, shredded cheese, diced green chilies, chopped cilantro, ground cumin, salt, and black pepper. Mix until well combined.
4. To assemble the enchiladas, spoon a generous amount of the prepared chicken filling onto each flour tortilla, then roll it up tightly and place it seam-side down in the prepared baking dish. Repeat with the remaining tortillas and filling.
5. Pour the prepared enchilada sauce evenly over the rolled-up tortillas in the baking dish. Sprinkle additional shredded cheese on top.
6. Cover the baking dish with aluminum foil and bake in the preheated oven for 20-25 minutes, or until the enchiladas are heated through and the cheese is melted and bubbly.
7. Remove the foil from the baking dish and garnish the enchiladas with chopped fresh cilantro.
8. Serve the spicy chicken enchiladas hot, with sour cream and sliced jalapeños on the side if desired.

Enjoy these delicious and flavorful spicy chicken enchiladas with your favorite toppings for a satisfying meal! Adjust the level of spice by increasing or decreasing the amount of cayenne pepper in the sauce.

Spicy Thai Coconut Soup (Tom Yum)

Ingredients:

- 4 cups chicken or vegetable broth
- 1 can (14 oz) coconut milk
- 1 stalk lemongrass, bruised and chopped into pieces
- 3-4 slices galangal or ginger
- 3-4 kaffir lime leaves, torn
- 2-3 red bird's eye chilies, sliced (adjust to taste)
- 2 tablespoons fish sauce
- 1 tablespoon soy sauce (optional)
- 1 tablespoon lime juice
- 1 teaspoon sugar
- 8-10 large shrimp, peeled and deveined
- 8-10 mushrooms, sliced
- 1 small tomato, cut into wedges
- Handful of fresh cilantro leaves, chopped
- Handful of Thai basil leaves, torn (optional)
- Salt to taste

Instructions:

1. In a large pot, bring the chicken or vegetable broth to a boil over medium-high heat.
2. Add the lemongrass, galangal or ginger, kaffir lime leaves, and sliced bird's eye chilies to the pot. Let it simmer for about 5-10 minutes to infuse the flavors into the broth.
3. Stir in the coconut milk, fish sauce, soy sauce (if using), lime juice, and sugar. Let the soup simmer for another 5 minutes.
4. Add the sliced mushrooms and tomato wedges to the pot. Cook for 2-3 minutes until the mushrooms are tender.
5. Add the shrimp to the pot and cook for another 2-3 minutes until they turn pink and opaque.
6. Taste the soup and adjust the seasoning with salt or additional fish sauce if needed.
7. Remove the pot from heat and discard the lemongrass, galangal or ginger, and kaffir lime leaves.

8. Ladle the hot and spicy Thai coconut soup into bowls. Garnish with chopped cilantro and torn Thai basil leaves, if desired.
9. Serve the Tom Yum soup hot as a comforting and flavorful appetizer or main dish.

Enjoy the bold and aromatic flavors of this Spicy Thai Coconut Soup, which perfectly balances the heat from the chilies with the creaminess of the coconut milk! Adjust the level of spiciness to your taste preference by adding more or fewer bird's eye chilies.

Spicy Korean Fried Chicken

Ingredients:

For the Chicken:

- 2 lbs (about 900g) chicken wings or drumsticks
- 1 cup buttermilk
- 1 cup all-purpose flour
- 1 teaspoon salt
- 1/2 teaspoon black pepper
- Vegetable oil for frying

For the Sauce:

- 1/4 cup gochujang (Korean chili paste)
- 2 tablespoons soy sauce
- 2 tablespoons honey
- 2 tablespoons rice vinegar
- 2 cloves garlic, minced
- 1 teaspoon grated ginger
- 1 tablespoon sesame oil
- 1 tablespoon toasted sesame seeds (for garnish)
- Sliced green onions (for garnish)

Instructions:

1. In a large bowl, marinate the chicken wings or drumsticks in buttermilk for at least 1 hour or overnight in the refrigerator. This helps tenderize the chicken and adds flavor.
2. In a shallow dish, combine the all-purpose flour, salt, and black pepper. Dredge each piece of chicken in the seasoned flour mixture, shaking off any excess.
3. In a deep skillet or Dutch oven, heat vegetable oil to 350°F (175°C). Carefully add the chicken to the hot oil in batches, making sure not to overcrowd the pan. Fry the chicken for about 10-12 minutes, or until golden brown and cooked through. Transfer the fried chicken to a wire rack or paper towel-lined plate to drain any excess oil.

4. While the chicken is frying, make the spicy Korean sauce. In a small saucepan, combine the gochujang, soy sauce, honey, rice vinegar, minced garlic, grated ginger, and sesame oil. Cook over low heat, stirring constantly, until the sauce is smooth and heated through.
5. Once all the chicken is fried, toss it in the spicy Korean sauce until evenly coated.
6. Transfer the coated chicken to a serving platter and garnish with toasted sesame seeds and sliced green onions.
7. Serve the spicy Korean fried chicken hot as a delicious appetizer or main dish.

Enjoy the crispy, spicy, and flavorful goodness of this Spicy Korean Fried Chicken! Adjust the level of heat by adding more or less gochujang according to your preference.

Spicy Salsa Verde

Ingredients:

- 1 lb (about 450g) tomatillos, husked and rinsed
- 2-3 jalapeño peppers (adjust to taste), stemmed and halved
- 1 small onion, peeled and quartered
- 2 cloves garlic, peeled
- 1/4 cup fresh cilantro leaves
- Juice of 1 lime
- Salt to taste

Instructions:

1. Preheat your broiler to high. Place the tomatillos, jalapeño peppers, onion quarters, and garlic cloves on a baking sheet.
2. Place the baking sheet under the broiler and broil for 5-7 minutes, turning occasionally, until the vegetables are charred and softened.
3. Remove the baking sheet from the broiler and let the vegetables cool slightly.
4. Once the vegetables are cool enough to handle, transfer them to a blender or food processor. Add the fresh cilantro leaves and lime juice.
5. Blend the mixture until smooth. If you prefer a chunkier salsa, pulse the mixture a few times until you reach your desired consistency.
6. Taste the salsa and season with salt to taste. Adjust the level of spiciness by adding more or fewer jalapeño peppers.
7. Transfer the salsa to a serving bowl and refrigerate for at least 30 minutes to allow the flavors to meld together.
8. Serve the spicy salsa verde with tortilla chips, tacos, quesadillas, or your favorite Mexican dishes.

Enjoy the vibrant flavors of this Spicy Salsa Verde as a zesty and flavorful addition to your meals or as a tasty dip! Adjust the level of heat by adding more or fewer jalapeño peppers, and customize the flavor by adjusting the amount of cilantro and lime juice to your preference.

Spicy Szechuan Eggplant

Ingredients:

- 2 medium-sized Chinese eggplants, sliced into bite-sized pieces
- 3 tablespoons vegetable oil
- 2 cloves garlic, minced
- 1-inch piece of ginger, minced
- 2 green onions, sliced (white and green parts separated)
- 2 tablespoons Szechuan peppercorns, crushed
- 2 tablespoons doubanjiang (fermented chili bean paste)
- 1 tablespoon soy sauce
- 1 tablespoon rice vinegar
- 1 tablespoon sugar
- 1/2 cup water
- 1 teaspoon cornstarch mixed with 1 tablespoon water (optional, for thickening)
- Toasted sesame seeds and sliced green onions for garnish

Instructions:

1. Heat the vegetable oil in a large skillet or wok over medium-high heat. Add the sliced eggplants to the skillet in a single layer and cook for about 2-3 minutes on each side until they are lightly browned and tender. Remove the cooked eggplants from the skillet and set aside.
2. In the same skillet, add a bit more oil if needed. Add the minced garlic, ginger, and the white parts of the sliced green onions. Stir-fry for about 1-2 minutes until fragrant.
3. Add the crushed Szechuan peppercorns and doubanjiang (fermented chili bean paste) to the skillet. Stir-fry for another minute to toast the spices and release their flavors.
4. Return the cooked eggplants to the skillet. Add the soy sauce, rice vinegar, sugar, and water to the skillet. Stir to combine everything.
5. Cover the skillet and let the eggplants simmer in the sauce for about 5-7 minutes, or until they are fully cooked and tender.
6. If desired, thicken the sauce with the cornstarch mixture by stirring it into the skillet. Cook for another minute until the sauce thickens slightly.
7. Remove the skillet from heat. Garnish the Spicy Szechuan Eggplant with toasted sesame seeds and the sliced green parts of the green onions.

8. Serve the Spicy Szechuan Eggplant hot over steamed rice or with noodles.

Enjoy the bold and spicy flavors of this Spicy Szechuan Eggplant dish, which pairs perfectly with rice or noodles for a satisfying meal! Adjust the level of spice to your preference by adding more or less chili bean paste and Szechuan peppercorns.

Spicy Tandoori Chicken

Ingredients:

- 2 lbs (about 900g) chicken pieces (bone-in and skin-on, such as thighs, drumsticks, or breast)
- 1 cup plain yogurt
- 3 tablespoons lemon juice
- 2 tablespoons vegetable oil
- 2 cloves garlic, minced
- 1 tablespoon grated ginger
- 1 tablespoon ground cumin
- 1 tablespoon ground coriander
- 1 tablespoon paprika
- 1 teaspoon turmeric
- 1 teaspoon chili powder (adjust to taste for desired spice level)
- 1 teaspoon garam masala
- Salt to taste
- Fresh cilantro leaves and lemon wedges for garnish

Instructions:

1. In a large bowl, combine the plain yogurt, lemon juice, vegetable oil, minced garlic, grated ginger, ground cumin, ground coriander, paprika, turmeric, chili powder, garam masala, and salt. Mix until well combined.
2. Add the chicken pieces to the bowl and toss to coat them evenly with the marinade. Cover the bowl with plastic wrap and refrigerate for at least 2 hours, or preferably overnight, to allow the flavors to meld and the chicken to marinate.
3. Preheat your grill to medium-high heat. If using an oven, preheat it to 425°F (220°C).
4. Remove the marinated chicken from the refrigerator and let it sit at room temperature for about 20-30 minutes.
5. If grilling, place the chicken pieces on the preheated grill. Grill the chicken for about 6-8 minutes on each side, or until cooked through and charred in spots. If using an oven, place the chicken on a baking sheet lined with aluminum foil and bake for 25-30 minutes, or until cooked through and golden brown.
6. Once cooked, transfer the Spicy Tandoori Chicken to a serving platter. Garnish with fresh cilantro leaves and lemon wedges.

7. Serve the Spicy Tandoori Chicken hot with naan bread, rice, or your favorite side dishes.

Enjoy the bold and flavorful taste of this Spicy Tandoori Chicken, which is perfect for grilling outdoors or baking in the oven for a delicious meal any time of the year! Adjust the amount of chili powder to your desired level of spiciness.

Spicy Chipotle Black Bean Tacos

Ingredients:

For the Chipotle Black Beans:

- 2 cans (15 oz each) black beans, drained and rinsed
- 1 chipotle pepper in adobo sauce, minced
- 2 cloves garlic, minced
- 1 teaspoon ground cumin
- 1 teaspoon smoked paprika
- Salt to taste
- 1 tablespoon vegetable oil

For the Tacos:

- 8-10 small corn or flour tortillas
- 1 cup shredded lettuce
- 1 cup diced tomatoes
- 1/2 cup diced red onion
- 1/2 cup crumbled feta or cotija cheese (optional)
- Fresh cilantro leaves for garnish
- Lime wedges for serving

Instructions:

1. Heat the vegetable oil in a large skillet over medium heat. Add the minced garlic and cook for about 1 minute until fragrant.
2. Add the minced chipotle pepper, ground cumin, and smoked paprika to the skillet. Stir to combine and cook for another minute to toast the spices.
3. Add the drained and rinsed black beans to the skillet. Season with salt to taste. Cook the beans for about 5-7 minutes, stirring occasionally, until heated through and well coated with the chipotle mixture.
4. While the beans are cooking, warm the tortillas according to package instructions.
5. To assemble the tacos, spoon a generous amount of the chipotle black beans onto each warmed tortilla. Top with shredded lettuce, diced tomatoes, diced red

onion, and crumbled feta or cotija cheese (if using). Garnish with fresh cilantro leaves.
6. Serve the Spicy Chipotle Black Bean Tacos hot with lime wedges on the side for squeezing over the tacos.

Enjoy the bold and spicy flavors of these Spicy Chipotle Black Bean Tacos, which are perfect for a quick and satisfying meal! Feel free to customize the toppings to your liking, adding avocado, salsa, sour cream, or any other favorite taco toppings.

Spicy Thai Peanut Noodles

Ingredients:

For the Peanut Sauce:

- 1/3 cup creamy peanut butter
- 3 tablespoons soy sauce
- 2 tablespoons rice vinegar
- 2 tablespoons sesame oil
- 2 tablespoons honey or maple syrup
- 2 cloves garlic, minced
- 1 tablespoon grated ginger
- 1 tablespoon Sriracha sauce (adjust to taste)
- 1 tablespoon lime juice
- 1/4 cup warm water, or more as needed

For the Noodles:

- 8 oz (about 225g) rice noodles or spaghetti
- 2 tablespoons vegetable oil
- 1 red bell pepper, thinly sliced
- 1 carrot, julienned or thinly sliced
- 1/2 cup shredded cabbage or chopped bok choy
- 2 green onions, sliced
- 1/4 cup chopped peanuts (for garnish)
- Fresh cilantro leaves for garnish
- Lime wedges for serving

Instructions:

1. Cook the rice noodles or spaghetti according to the package instructions until al dente. Drain and rinse under cold water to stop the cooking process. Set aside.
2. In a small bowl, whisk together all the ingredients for the peanut sauce until smooth. Add more warm water as needed to achieve your desired consistency. Set aside.
3. Heat the vegetable oil in a large skillet or wok over medium-high heat. Add the sliced red bell pepper, julienned carrot, and shredded cabbage or chopped bok choy to the skillet. Stir-fry for 3-4 minutes until the vegetables are tender-crisp.

4. Add the cooked noodles to the skillet along with the prepared peanut sauce. Toss everything together until the noodles and vegetables are evenly coated with the sauce. Cook for an additional 2-3 minutes to heat through.
5. Remove the skillet from heat. Serve the Spicy Thai Peanut Noodles hot, garnished with sliced green onions, chopped peanuts, and fresh cilantro leaves. Serve with lime wedges on the side for squeezing over the noodles.

Enjoy the bold and spicy flavors of these Spicy Thai Peanut Noodles as a delicious and satisfying meal! Adjust the level of spiciness by adding more or less Sriracha sauce according to your preference. Feel free to customize the vegetables based on what you have on hand or your personal taste.

Spicy Cajun Dirty Rice

Ingredients:

- 1 cup long-grain white rice
- 2 cups chicken or vegetable broth
- 1 tablespoon vegetable oil
- 1 onion, finely chopped
- 1 bell pepper, finely chopped
- 2 celery stalks, finely chopped
- 2 cloves garlic, minced
- 8 oz (about 225g) ground pork or beef
- 8 oz (about 225g) chicken livers, finely chopped
- 2 teaspoons Cajun seasoning
- 1/2 teaspoon paprika
- 1/4 teaspoon cayenne pepper (adjust to taste)
- Salt and black pepper to taste
- 2 green onions, thinly sliced (for garnish)
- Chopped fresh parsley (for garnish)

Instructions:

1. Rinse the rice under cold water until the water runs clear. Drain and set aside.
2. In a medium saucepan, bring the chicken or vegetable broth to a boil. Stir in the rice, reduce the heat to low, cover, and simmer for 18-20 minutes, or until the rice is cooked and the liquid is absorbed. Remove from heat and let it sit, covered, for 5 minutes. Fluff the rice with a fork and set aside.
3. In a large skillet, heat the vegetable oil over medium heat. Add the chopped onion, bell pepper, and celery. Cook, stirring occasionally, for about 5-7 minutes, or until the vegetables are softened.
4. Add the minced garlic to the skillet and cook for another minute until fragrant.
5. Push the vegetables to one side of the skillet and add the ground pork or beef to the other side. Cook, breaking it up with a spoon, until browned and cooked through.
6. Stir in the chopped chicken livers and cook for 5-7 minutes, or until they are cooked through and no longer pink.
7. Season the mixture with Cajun seasoning, paprika, cayenne pepper, salt, and black pepper. Stir to combine everything evenly.

8. Add the cooked rice to the skillet and stir to combine with the meat and vegetable mixture. Cook for another 3-5 minutes, or until everything is heated through and well combined.
9. Remove the skillet from heat. Garnish the Spicy Cajun Dirty Rice with thinly sliced green onions and chopped fresh parsley before serving.

Enjoy the bold and flavorful taste of this Spicy Cajun Dirty Rice as a hearty and satisfying dish! Adjust the level of spiciness by adding more or less cayenne pepper according to your preference.

Spicy Mango Chicken Curry

Ingredients:

- 1 lb (about 450g) boneless, skinless chicken breasts or thighs, cut into bite-sized pieces
- 2 tablespoons vegetable oil
- 1 onion, finely chopped
- 2 cloves garlic, minced
- 1 tablespoon grated ginger
- 1 red bell pepper, chopped
- 1 mango, peeled, pitted, and diced
- 1 can (14 oz) coconut milk
- 2 tablespoons red curry paste
- 1 tablespoon curry powder
- 1 teaspoon ground turmeric
- 1 teaspoon ground cumin
- 1 teaspoon ground coriander
- 1/2 teaspoon cayenne pepper (adjust to taste)
- Salt and black pepper to taste
- 1 tablespoon brown sugar or honey (optional, for sweetness)
- Juice of 1 lime
- Chopped fresh cilantro for garnish
- Cooked rice or naan bread for serving

Instructions:

1. Heat the vegetable oil in a large skillet or Dutch oven over medium heat. Add the chopped onion and cook for 3-4 minutes until softened.
2. Add the minced garlic and grated ginger to the skillet. Cook for another minute until fragrant.
3. Add the chopped red bell pepper to the skillet and cook for 2-3 minutes until slightly softened.
4. Push the vegetables to one side of the skillet and add the chicken pieces to the other side. Cook the chicken until browned on all sides, about 5-6 minutes.
5. Stir in the red curry paste, curry powder, ground turmeric, ground cumin, ground coriander, and cayenne pepper. Cook for 1-2 minutes until the spices are fragrant.
6. Add the diced mango and coconut milk to the skillet. Stir to combine everything evenly.

7. Season the curry with salt and black pepper to taste. If you prefer a sweeter curry, add brown sugar or honey at this point.
8. Bring the curry to a simmer and let it cook for 15-20 minutes, stirring occasionally, until the chicken is cooked through and the sauce has thickened slightly.
9. Remove the skillet from heat and stir in the lime juice. Taste and adjust the seasoning if needed.
10. Serve the Spicy Mango Chicken Curry hot over cooked rice or with naan bread. Garnish with chopped fresh cilantro before serving.

Enjoy the bold and exotic flavors of this Spicy Mango Chicken Curry as a delicious and satisfying meal! Adjust the level of spiciness by adding more or less cayenne pepper according to your preference.

Spicy Korean Kimchi

Ingredients:

- 1 napa cabbage
- 1/4 cup coarse sea salt
- 1 cup Korean red pepper powder (gochugaru)
- 1/4 cup fish sauce or soy sauce for a vegetarian option
- 1 tablespoon grated ginger
- 4 cloves garlic, minced
- 2 tablespoons sugar
- 4 green onions, chopped
- 1 carrot, julienned
- 1 daikon radish, julienned (optional)

Instructions:

1. Cut the napa cabbage into quarters lengthwise, then chop it into bite-sized pieces. Rinse the cabbage pieces under cold water and drain.
2. In a large bowl, dissolve the coarse sea salt in 8 cups of water. Submerge the cabbage pieces in the salt water and let them soak for 2 hours, turning occasionally.
3. While the cabbage is soaking, prepare the seasoning paste. In a separate bowl, mix together the Korean red pepper powder, fish sauce (or soy sauce), grated ginger, minced garlic, and sugar until well combined.
4. After 2 hours, rinse the cabbage pieces under cold water to remove excess salt. Drain well and squeeze out any excess water.
5. In a large mixing bowl, combine the drained cabbage pieces with the seasoning paste. Add the chopped green onions, julienned carrot, and daikon radish (if using). Mix everything together until the cabbage is evenly coated with the seasoning paste.
6. Pack the seasoned cabbage mixture tightly into clean glass jars, pressing down firmly to remove any air pockets.
7. Leave the jars of kimchi at room temperature for 1-2 days to ferment, then transfer them to the refrigerator. The kimchi will continue to ferment and develop flavor over time.
8. Serve the Spicy Korean Kimchi as a side dish with rice, noodles, or as a topping for sandwiches and wraps.

Enjoy the bold and tangy flavors of homemade Spicy Korean Kimchi, which is packed with probiotics and nutrients! Adjust the level of spiciness by adding more or less Korean red pepper powder according to your preference.

Spicy Buffalo Chicken Dip

Ingredients:

- 2 cups shredded cooked chicken (rotisserie chicken works well)
- 8 oz (about 225g) cream cheese, softened
- 1/2 cup ranch dressing
- 1/2 cup hot sauce (such as Frank's RedHot)
- 1/2 cup shredded cheddar cheese
- 1/4 cup crumbled blue cheese (optional)
- 1/4 cup chopped green onions (optional)
- Tortilla chips, celery sticks, or carrot sticks for serving

Instructions:

1. Preheat your oven to 350°F (175°C).
2. In a large mixing bowl, combine the shredded cooked chicken, softened cream cheese, ranch dressing, and hot sauce. Mix until well combined.
3. Stir in the shredded cheddar cheese, crumbled blue cheese (if using), and chopped green onions (if using). Mix until all ingredients are evenly distributed.
4. Transfer the mixture to a baking dish or oven-safe skillet, spreading it out into an even layer.
5. Bake in the preheated oven for 20-25 minutes, or until the dip is hot and bubbly around the edges.
6. Remove the dip from the oven and let it cool for a few minutes before serving.
7. Garnish the Spicy Buffalo Chicken Dip with additional chopped green onions, if desired.
8. Serve the dip warm with tortilla chips, celery sticks, or carrot sticks for dipping.

Enjoy the creamy and spicy flavors of this Spicy Buffalo Chicken Dip, perfect for parties, game days, or any occasion! Adjust the level of spiciness by adding more or less hot sauce according to your preference.

Spicy Jalapeno Cornbread

Ingredients:

- 1 cup yellow cornmeal
- 1 cup all-purpose flour
- 1 tablespoon baking powder
- 1 teaspoon salt
- 1/4 cup granulated sugar
- 1 cup buttermilk
- 2 large eggs
- 1/4 cup unsalted butter, melted
- 1/4 cup vegetable oil
- 1 cup canned corn kernels, drained
- 2-3 jalapeño peppers, seeded and finely chopped
- 1 cup shredded cheddar cheese (optional)
- 1/4 cup chopped fresh cilantro (optional)

Instructions:

1. Preheat your oven to 400°F (200°C). Grease a 9-inch square baking dish or cast iron skillet with butter or oil.
2. In a large mixing bowl, combine the yellow cornmeal, all-purpose flour, baking powder, salt, and granulated sugar.
3. In a separate bowl, whisk together the buttermilk, eggs, melted butter, and vegetable oil until well combined.
4. Pour the wet ingredients into the dry ingredients and stir until just combined. Do not overmix.
5. Fold in the canned corn kernels, chopped jalapeño peppers, shredded cheddar cheese (if using), and chopped fresh cilantro (if using) until evenly distributed throughout the batter.
6. Pour the batter into the prepared baking dish or skillet, spreading it out into an even layer.
7. Bake in the preheated oven for 20-25 minutes, or until the cornbread is golden brown and a toothpick inserted into the center comes out clean.
8. Remove the cornbread from the oven and let it cool for a few minutes before slicing and serving.

9. Serve the Spicy Jalapeño Cornbread warm as a side dish with chili, barbecue, or any meal of your choice.

Enjoy the deliciously spicy and flavorful Spicy Jalapeño Cornbread, perfect for adding a kick to your meals! Adjust the level of spiciness by adding more or fewer jalapeño peppers according to your preference.

Spicy Singapore Noodles

Ingredients:

- 8 oz (about 225g) rice vermicelli noodles
- 2 tablespoons vegetable oil
- 2 cloves garlic, minced
- 1 tablespoon grated ginger
- 1 onion, thinly sliced
- 1 red bell pepper, thinly sliced
- 1 green bell pepper, thinly sliced
- 1 carrot, julienned
- 1 cup shredded cabbage
- 1 cup bean sprouts
- 2 green onions, sliced
- 2 eggs, lightly beaten
- 1/4 cup soy sauce
- 2 tablespoons curry powder
- 1 tablespoon chili garlic sauce or Sriracha (adjust to taste)
- Salt and black pepper to taste
- Fresh cilantro leaves for garnish
- Lime wedges for serving

Instructions:

1. Cook the rice vermicelli noodles according to the package instructions until al dente. Drain and rinse under cold water to stop the cooking process. Set aside.
2. In a large skillet or wok, heat the vegetable oil over medium-high heat. Add the minced garlic and grated ginger to the skillet. Cook for 1-2 minutes until fragrant.
3. Add the thinly sliced onion, red bell pepper, green bell pepper, and julienned carrot to the skillet. Stir-fry for 3-4 minutes until the vegetables are slightly softened.
4. Push the vegetables to one side of the skillet and pour the beaten eggs into the other side. Scramble the eggs until cooked through, then mix them with the vegetables.
5. Add the shredded cabbage and bean sprouts to the skillet. Stir-fry for another 2-3 minutes until the vegetables are tender-crisp.
6. In a small bowl, mix together the soy sauce, curry powder, and chili garlic sauce or Sriracha until well combined.

7. Pour the sauce mixture over the vegetables and noodles in the skillet. Toss everything together until evenly coated with the sauce.
8. Season the Spicy Singapore Noodles with salt and black pepper to taste. Adjust the level of spiciness by adding more or less chili garlic sauce or Sriracha according to your preference.
9. Remove the skillet from heat and garnish the Spicy Singapore Noodles with sliced green onions and fresh cilantro leaves.
10. Serve the noodles hot with lime wedges on the side for squeezing over the noodles.

Enjoy the bold and spicy flavors of these Spicy Singapore Noodles as a delicious and satisfying meal! Customize the recipe by adding your favorite protein such as shrimp, chicken, or tofu.

Spicy Sriracha Deviled Eggs

Ingredients:

- 6 large eggs
- 2 tablespoons mayonnaise
- 1 tablespoon Sriracha sauce (adjust to taste)
- 1 teaspoon Dijon mustard
- 1/4 teaspoon garlic powder
- Salt and black pepper to taste
- Paprika, for garnish
- Fresh chives or green onions, chopped (optional, for garnish)

Instructions:

1. Place the eggs in a single layer in a saucepan and cover them with water. Bring the water to a boil over medium-high heat.
2. Once the water reaches a rolling boil, cover the saucepan with a lid and remove it from heat. Let the eggs sit in the hot water for 10-12 minutes.
3. While the eggs are boiling, prepare an ice water bath in a large bowl.
4. After 10-12 minutes, use a slotted spoon to transfer the boiled eggs to the ice water bath to cool completely. Let them sit in the ice water for about 5 minutes.
5. Once cooled, carefully peel the eggs and slice them in half lengthwise. Remove the yolks and place them in a separate bowl.
6. Mash the egg yolks with a fork until they are crumbly.
7. Add the mayonnaise, Sriracha sauce, Dijon mustard, garlic powder, salt, and black pepper to the mashed egg yolks. Mix until smooth and creamy. Adjust the amount of Sriracha sauce to your desired level of spiciness.
8. Spoon or pipe the spicy Sriracha mixture into the hollowed-out egg whites.
9. Sprinkle the deviled eggs with paprika for color.
10. Garnish the Spicy Sriracha Deviled Eggs with chopped fresh chives or green onions, if desired.
11. Chill the deviled eggs in the refrigerator for at least 30 minutes before serving to allow the flavors to meld together.

Enjoy the deliciously spicy and creamy Spicy Sriracha Deviled Eggs as a tasty appetizer or snack! Adjust the level of spiciness to your preference by adding more or less Sriracha sauce.

Spicy Chicken Tortilla Soup

Ingredients:

- 1 tablespoon olive oil
- 1 onion, diced
- 2 cloves garlic, minced
- 1 jalapeño pepper, seeded and diced
- 1 red bell pepper, diced
- 1 green bell pepper, diced
- 1 carrot, diced
- 1 teaspoon ground cumin
- 1 teaspoon chili powder
- 1/2 teaspoon smoked paprika
- 1/4 teaspoon cayenne pepper (adjust to taste)
- Salt and black pepper to taste
- 4 cups chicken broth
- 1 can (14.5 oz) diced tomatoes
- 1 cup frozen corn kernels
- 1 can (15 oz) black beans, drained and rinsed
- 2 cups cooked shredded chicken
- Juice of 1 lime
- 1/4 cup chopped fresh cilantro
- Tortilla chips, avocado slices, lime wedges, and sour cream for serving

Instructions:

1. In a large pot or Dutch oven, heat the olive oil over medium heat. Add the diced onion and cook for 2-3 minutes until softened.
2. Add the minced garlic, diced jalapeño pepper, diced red bell pepper, diced green bell pepper, and diced carrot to the pot. Cook for another 5 minutes until the vegetables are tender.
3. Stir in the ground cumin, chili powder, smoked paprika, cayenne pepper, salt, and black pepper. Cook for 1-2 minutes until the spices are fragrant.
4. Pour in the chicken broth and diced tomatoes with their juices. Bring the soup to a simmer and let it cook for 10-15 minutes to allow the flavors to meld together.

5. Add the frozen corn kernels, drained and rinsed black beans, and cooked shredded chicken to the pot. Stir to combine and cook for another 5-10 minutes until heated through.
6. Stir in the lime juice and chopped fresh cilantro. Taste and adjust the seasoning if needed.
7. Serve the Spicy Chicken Tortilla Soup hot, garnished with crushed tortilla chips, avocado slices, lime wedges, and a dollop of sour cream.

Enjoy the bold and flavorful Spicy Chicken Tortilla Soup, topped with your favorite garnishes for added texture and freshness! Adjust the level of spiciness by adding more or less cayenne pepper according to your preference.

Spicy Chipotle Hummus

Ingredients:

- 1 can (15 oz) chickpeas, drained and rinsed
- 2 tablespoons tahini
- 2 tablespoons extra virgin olive oil
- 2 tablespoons fresh lemon juice
- 1-2 chipotle peppers in adobo sauce (adjust to taste)
- 2 cloves garlic, minced
- 1 teaspoon ground cumin
- 1/2 teaspoon smoked paprika
- Salt to taste
- 2-4 tablespoons water (as needed for consistency)
- Fresh cilantro leaves for garnish (optional)
- Extra virgin olive oil for drizzling (optional)

Instructions:

1. In a food processor, combine the drained and rinsed chickpeas, tahini, extra virgin olive oil, fresh lemon juice, chipotle peppers in adobo sauce, minced garlic, ground cumin, smoked paprika, and a pinch of salt.
2. Blend the ingredients until smooth, scraping down the sides of the bowl as needed. If the hummus is too thick, add water, 1 tablespoon at a time, until you reach your desired consistency.
3. Taste the hummus and adjust the seasoning as needed. Add more chipotle peppers for extra heat or more lemon juice for acidity.
4. Once the hummus reaches the desired consistency and flavor, transfer it to a serving bowl.
5. Garnish the Spicy Chipotle Hummus with fresh cilantro leaves and a drizzle of extra virgin olive oil, if desired.
6. Serve the hummus with pita bread, tortilla chips, vegetable sticks, or crackers for dipping.

Enjoy the bold and spicy flavors of this Spicy Chipotle Hummus as a delicious dip or spread! Adjust the level of spiciness by adding more or fewer chipotle peppers according to your preference.

Spicy Thai Basil Beef

Ingredients:

- 1 lb (about 450g) flank steak or sirloin steak, thinly sliced against the grain
- 2 tablespoons vegetable oil
- 4 cloves garlic, minced
- 2 Thai bird's eye chilies, thinly sliced (adjust to taste)
- 1 red bell pepper, thinly sliced
- 1 yellow bell pepper, thinly sliced
- 1 onion, thinly sliced
- 1 cup fresh basil leaves, loosely packed
- 2 tablespoons oyster sauce
- 1 tablespoon soy sauce
- 1 tablespoon fish sauce
- 1 tablespoon brown sugar
- 1/2 teaspoon ground black pepper
- Cooked rice, for serving

Instructions:

1. Heat the vegetable oil in a large skillet or wok over high heat.
2. Add the minced garlic and sliced Thai bird's eye chilies to the skillet. Stir-fry for 30 seconds to 1 minute until fragrant.
3. Add the thinly sliced steak to the skillet in a single layer. Let it sear without stirring for 1-2 minutes until browned on one side, then stir-fry for another 1-2 minutes until almost cooked through. Remove the beef from the skillet and set aside.
4. In the same skillet, add the thinly sliced red and yellow bell peppers and sliced onion. Stir-fry for 2-3 minutes until slightly softened.
5. Return the cooked beef to the skillet. Add the oyster sauce, soy sauce, fish sauce, brown sugar, and ground black pepper. Stir to combine all the ingredients.
6. Cook for another 1-2 minutes until the beef is cooked through and the sauce has thickened slightly.
7. Add the fresh basil leaves to the skillet and toss everything together until the basil wilts.
8. Remove the skillet from heat. Taste and adjust the seasoning if needed.
9. Serve the Spicy Thai Basil Beef hot over cooked rice.

Enjoy the bold and aromatic flavors of this Spicy Thai Basil Beef, which pairs perfectly with steamed rice for a satisfying meal! Adjust the level of spiciness by adding more or fewer Thai bird's eye chilies according to your preference.

Spicy Cajun Crab Cakes

Ingredients:

- 1 lb (about 450g) lump crabmeat, drained
- 1/2 cup breadcrumbs
- 1/4 cup mayonnaise
- 1 large egg, beaten
- 2 green onions, thinly sliced
- 1/4 cup red bell pepper, finely diced
- 1/4 cup celery, finely diced
- 1 tablespoon fresh parsley, chopped
- 1 tablespoon fresh lemon juice
- 1 teaspoon Cajun seasoning
- 1/2 teaspoon smoked paprika
- 1/4 teaspoon cayenne pepper (adjust to taste)
- Salt and black pepper to taste
- 2 tablespoons vegetable oil, for frying

Instructions:

1. In a large mixing bowl, combine the lump crabmeat, breadcrumbs, mayonnaise, beaten egg, sliced green onions, diced red bell pepper, diced celery, chopped parsley, fresh lemon juice, Cajun seasoning, smoked paprika, cayenne pepper, salt, and black pepper. Gently mix until all ingredients are well combined.
2. Divide the crab mixture into equal portions and shape them into patties using your hands. Place the formed crab cakes on a baking sheet lined with parchment paper.
3. Heat the vegetable oil in a large skillet over medium heat.
4. Once the oil is hot, carefully add the crab cakes to the skillet in batches, making sure not to overcrowd the pan. Cook the crab cakes for 3-4 minutes on each side, or until golden brown and crispy.
5. Transfer the cooked crab cakes to a plate lined with paper towels to drain any excess oil.
6. Serve the Spicy Cajun Crab Cakes hot, garnished with additional chopped parsley and lemon wedges on the side for squeezing.

Enjoy the deliciously spicy and flavorful Spicy Cajun Crab Cakes as an appetizer or main dish! Adjust the level of spiciness by adding more or less cayenne pepper according to your preference.

Spicy Szechuan Green Beans

Ingredients:

- 1 lb (about 450g) green beans, washed and trimmed
- 2 tablespoons vegetable oil
- 3 cloves garlic, minced
- 1 tablespoon fresh ginger, minced
- 2-3 dried red chilies, chopped (adjust to taste)
- 2 green onions, chopped
- 2 tablespoons soy sauce
- 1 tablespoon hoisin sauce
- 1 tablespoon rice vinegar
- 1 tablespoon sesame oil
- 1 teaspoon sugar
- 1 teaspoon Szechuan peppercorns, crushed
- Salt to taste
- Toasted sesame seeds for garnish (optional)

Instructions:

1. Blanch the green beans in a pot of boiling water for 2-3 minutes until they are bright green and slightly tender. Drain and set aside.
2. In a large skillet or wok, heat the vegetable oil over medium-high heat.
3. Add the minced garlic, minced ginger, and chopped dried red chilies to the skillet. Stir-fry for 1-2 minutes until fragrant.
4. Add the blanched green beans to the skillet, along with the chopped green onions. Stir-fry for another 2-3 minutes until the green beans are cooked through and tender-crisp.
5. In a small bowl, whisk together the soy sauce, hoisin sauce, rice vinegar, sesame oil, sugar, crushed Szechuan peppercorns, and a pinch of salt.
6. Pour the sauce mixture over the green beans in the skillet. Stir to coat the green beans evenly with the sauce.
7. Cook for another 1-2 minutes until the sauce has thickened slightly and coats the green beans.
8. Remove the skillet from heat and transfer the Spicy Szechuan Green Beans to a serving dish.
9. Garnish with toasted sesame seeds, if desired.
10. Serve the Spicy Szechuan Green Beans hot as a flavorful side dish.

Enjoy the bold and spicy flavors of these Spicy Szechuan Green Beans! Adjust the level of spiciness by adding more or fewer dried red chilies according to your preference.

Spicy Korean Bibimbap

Ingredients:

For the Bibimbap Sauce:

- 1/4 cup gochujang (Korean red chili paste)
- 2 tablespoons soy sauce
- 1 tablespoon sesame oil
- 1 tablespoon honey or brown sugar
- 1 tablespoon rice vinegar
- 1 clove garlic, minced
- 1 teaspoon grated ginger

For the Bibimbap:

- 2 cups cooked short-grain white rice
- 1 tablespoon vegetable oil
- 1 carrot, julienned
- 1 zucchini, julienned
- 1 cup fresh spinach leaves
- 4 oz (about 115g) shiitake mushrooms, sliced
- 2 cups bean sprouts
- 2 cups cooked protein of your choice (such as beef, chicken, tofu, or shrimp)
- 4 large eggs
- Toasted sesame seeds, for garnish
- Thinly sliced green onions, for garnish

Instructions:

1. In a small bowl, mix together all the ingredients for the Bibimbap sauce until well combined. Set aside.
2. Divide the cooked rice evenly among four serving bowls.
3. Heat the vegetable oil in a large skillet over medium heat. Add the julienned carrot and zucchini to the skillet. Stir-fry for 2-3 minutes until slightly softened. Remove from the skillet and set aside.

4. In the same skillet, add the fresh spinach leaves. Cook for 1-2 minutes until wilted. Remove from the skillet and set aside.
5. Add the sliced shiitake mushrooms to the skillet. Stir-fry for 3-4 minutes until golden brown and tender. Remove from the skillet and set aside.
6. Add the bean sprouts to the skillet. Stir-fry for 2-3 minutes until heated through. Remove from the skillet and set aside.
7. In the same skillet, cook the eggs sunny-side-up or over-easy, according to your preference.
8. To assemble the Bibimbap, arrange the cooked vegetables and protein over the rice in each serving bowl. Place a cooked egg on top of each bowl.
9. Drizzle the Bibimbap sauce over each bowl.
10. Garnish with toasted sesame seeds and thinly sliced green onions.
11. Serve the Spicy Korean Bibimbap immediately, mixing everything together before eating.

Enjoy the deliciously spicy and flavorful Spicy Korean Bibimbap as a satisfying and nutritious meal! Adjust the level of spiciness by adding more or less gochujang according to your preference.

Spicy Mango Habanero Salsa

Ingredients:

- 2 ripe mangoes, peeled, pitted, and diced
- 1-2 habanero peppers, seeded and finely diced (adjust to taste)
- 1/4 cup red onion, finely chopped
- 1/4 cup fresh cilantro, chopped
- Juice of 1 lime
- Salt to taste

Instructions:

1. In a mixing bowl, combine the diced mangoes, finely diced habanero peppers, chopped red onion, and chopped cilantro.
2. Squeeze the juice of one lime over the ingredients in the bowl.
3. Stir everything together until well combined.
4. Taste the salsa and add salt as needed, adjusting to your preference.
5. Transfer the Spicy Mango Habanero Salsa to a serving bowl.
6. Serve immediately or refrigerate for at least 30 minutes to allow the flavors to meld together before serving.
7. Enjoy the Spicy Mango Habanero Salsa as a dip with tortilla chips, or as a topping for grilled chicken, fish, tacos, or salads.

This salsa is sweet, spicy, and tangy, with the fruity flavor of mangoes complementing the fiery heat of habanero peppers. Adjust the amount of habanero peppers according to your tolerance for heat.

Spicy Buffalo Chicken Sliders

Ingredients:

For the Buffalo Chicken:

- 1 lb (about 450g) boneless, skinless chicken breasts or thighs
- 1/2 cup buffalo sauce (such as Frank's RedHot)
- 2 tablespoons unsalted butter, melted
- 1 teaspoon garlic powder
- Salt and black pepper to taste

For the Sliders:

- 8 slider buns
- 1 cup coleslaw mix
- 1/4 cup blue cheese dressing or ranch dressing
- 1/4 cup crumbled blue cheese (optional)
- Sliced green onions or chopped fresh parsley for garnish (optional)

Instructions:

1. Preheat your oven to 375°F (190°C). Line a baking sheet with parchment paper or aluminum foil.
2. Season the chicken breasts or thighs with salt, black pepper, and garlic powder on both sides.
3. In a small bowl, mix together the buffalo sauce and melted butter.
4. Brush both sides of the chicken with the buffalo sauce mixture, reserving some for later use.
5. Place the chicken on the prepared baking sheet and bake in the preheated oven for 20-25 minutes, or until cooked through and no longer pink in the center. Remove from the oven and let it rest for a few minutes.
6. While the chicken is resting, lightly toast the slider buns in a toaster or on a skillet.
7. Slice the cooked chicken into smaller pieces to fit onto the slider buns.
8. In a separate bowl, toss the coleslaw mix with the blue cheese dressing until evenly coated.
9. Assemble the sliders by placing a piece of buffalo chicken on the bottom half of each slider bun.

10. Top the chicken with a spoonful of the coleslaw mixture.
11. Drizzle some of the reserved buffalo sauce mixture over the coleslaw.
12. If desired, sprinkle crumbled blue cheese, sliced green onions, or chopped fresh parsley on top.
13. Place the top half of the slider buns on each sandwich.
14. Secure each slider with a toothpick if necessary.
15. Serve the Spicy Buffalo Chicken Sliders immediately, and enjoy!

These Spicy Buffalo Chicken Sliders are perfect for game days, parties, or quick weeknight dinners. Adjust the level of spiciness by adding more or less buffalo sauce according to your preference.

Spicy Jalapeno Mac and Cheese

Ingredients:

- 8 oz (about 225g) elbow macaroni or pasta of your choice
- 2 tablespoons unsalted butter
- 2 tablespoons all-purpose flour
- 2 cups milk
- 2 cups shredded sharp cheddar cheese
- 1 cup shredded Monterey Jack cheese
- 1-2 jalapeño peppers, seeded and finely chopped (adjust to taste)
- 1/4 cup pickled jalapeños, chopped
- 1/4 teaspoon cayenne pepper (optional, for extra heat)
- Salt and black pepper to taste
- 1/2 cup breadcrumbs
- 2 tablespoons grated Parmesan cheese
- Chopped fresh cilantro or parsley for garnish (optional)

Instructions:

1. Preheat your oven to 375°F (190°C). Grease a 9x13-inch baking dish or individual ramekins.
2. Cook the elbow macaroni according to the package instructions until al dente. Drain and set aside.
3. In a large saucepan, melt the butter over medium heat. Add the flour and whisk continuously for 1-2 minutes to make a roux.
4. Slowly pour in the milk while whisking constantly to prevent lumps from forming.
5. Cook the sauce, stirring frequently, until it thickens and coats the back of a spoon, about 5-7 minutes.
6. Reduce the heat to low and stir in the shredded cheddar cheese and Monterey Jack cheese until melted and smooth.
7. Add the chopped jalapeño peppers, pickled jalapeños, cayenne pepper (if using), salt, and black pepper to the cheese sauce. Stir until well combined.
8. Add the cooked macaroni to the cheese sauce and stir until the pasta is evenly coated with the cheese mixture.
9. Transfer the mac and cheese mixture to the prepared baking dish or individual ramekins, spreading it out into an even layer.

10. In a small bowl, mix together the breadcrumbs and grated Parmesan cheese. Sprinkle the breadcrumb mixture evenly over the top of the mac and cheese.
11. Bake in the preheated oven for 20-25 minutes, or until the top is golden brown and the cheese is bubbly.
12. Remove from the oven and let it cool for a few minutes before serving.
13. Garnish with chopped fresh cilantro or parsley, if desired.
14. Serve the Spicy Jalapeño Mac and Cheese hot as a delicious and comforting meal or side dish.

Enjoy the creamy and spicy flavors of this Spicy Jalapeño Mac and Cheese, perfect for satisfying your comfort food cravings! Adjust the level of spiciness by adding more or fewer jalapeño peppers according to your preference.

Spicy Thai Green Curry

Ingredients:

- 1 lb (about 450g) boneless chicken thighs or tofu, cut into bite-sized pieces
- 2 tablespoons vegetable oil
- 3 tablespoons green curry paste
- 1 can (14 oz) coconut milk
- 1 cup chicken broth or vegetable broth
- 1 tablespoon fish sauce (optional, omit for vegetarian/vegan)
- 1 tablespoon brown sugar or palm sugar
- 1 cup mixed vegetables (such as bell peppers, bamboo shoots, green beans, and eggplant)
- 1 cup Thai basil leaves, torn
- 1-2 Thai bird's eye chilies, thinly sliced (adjust to taste)
- Juice of 1 lime
- Cooked rice, for serving

Instructions:

1. Heat the vegetable oil in a large skillet or wok over medium heat.
2. Add the green curry paste to the skillet and stir-fry for 1-2 minutes until fragrant.
3. Add the chicken or tofu pieces to the skillet and cook until browned on all sides.
4. Pour in the coconut milk and chicken broth, stirring to combine.
5. Stir in the fish sauce (if using) and brown sugar. Bring the mixture to a simmer.
6. Add the mixed vegetables to the skillet and simmer for 8-10 minutes until the vegetables are tender and the chicken is cooked through (if using).
7. Stir in the torn Thai basil leaves and sliced Thai bird's eye chilies.
8. Squeeze the lime juice over the curry and stir to combine.
9. Taste the curry and adjust the seasoning if needed, adding more fish sauce, sugar, or lime juice to balance the flavors.
10. Remove the skillet from heat.
11. Serve the Spicy Thai Green Curry hot over cooked rice.

Enjoy the bold and aromatic flavors of this Spicy Thai Green Curry! Adjust the level of spiciness by adding more or fewer Thai bird's eye chilies according to your preference.

Feel free to customize the vegetables and protein according to what you have on hand or your personal taste preferences.

Spicy Cajun Chicken Pasta

Ingredients:

- 8 oz (about 225g) penne pasta or pasta of your choice
- 2 boneless, skinless chicken breasts, cut into bite-sized pieces
- 2 tablespoons Cajun seasoning
- 2 tablespoons olive oil
- 2 tablespoons unsalted butter
- 1 red bell pepper, sliced
- 1 green bell pepper, sliced
- 1 small onion, thinly sliced
- 3 cloves garlic, minced
- 1 cup heavy cream
- 1/2 cup chicken broth
- 1/4 cup grated Parmesan cheese
- Salt and black pepper to taste
- Chopped fresh parsley for garnish

Instructions:

1. Cook the penne pasta according to the package instructions until al dente. Drain and set aside.
2. Season the chicken breast pieces with Cajun seasoning, making sure they are evenly coated.
3. Heat the olive oil in a large skillet over medium-high heat. Add the seasoned chicken pieces to the skillet and cook for 6-8 minutes, or until cooked through and browned on all sides. Remove the chicken from the skillet and set aside.
4. In the same skillet, melt the butter over medium heat. Add the sliced red bell pepper, green bell pepper, and thinly sliced onion. Cook for 3-4 minutes until the vegetables are tender.
5. Add the minced garlic to the skillet and cook for another 1-2 minutes until fragrant.
6. Pour in the heavy cream and chicken broth, stirring to combine. Bring the mixture to a simmer.
7. Reduce the heat to low and stir in the grated Parmesan cheese until melted and the sauce has thickened slightly.
8. Season the sauce with salt and black pepper to taste.

9. Return the cooked chicken to the skillet and stir to coat it evenly with the sauce.
10. Add the cooked penne pasta to the skillet and toss everything together until the pasta is coated with the sauce.
11. Cook for another 2-3 minutes until everything is heated through.
12. Remove the skillet from heat and garnish with chopped fresh parsley.
13. Serve the Spicy Cajun Chicken Pasta hot, garnished with additional grated Parmesan cheese if desired.

Enjoy the flavorful and spicy Spicy Cajun Chicken Pasta as a comforting and satisfying meal! Adjust the level of spiciness by adding more or less Cajun seasoning according to your preference.

Spicy Chipotle Lime Shrimp

Ingredients:

- 1 lb (about 450g) large shrimp, peeled and deveined
- 2 tablespoons olive oil
- 2 chipotle peppers in adobo sauce, finely chopped
- 3 cloves garlic, minced
- Zest and juice of 1 lime
- 1 teaspoon ground cumin
- 1 teaspoon smoked paprika
- 1/2 teaspoon chili powder
- Salt and black pepper to taste
- Chopped fresh cilantro for garnish
- Lime wedges for serving

Instructions:

1. In a mixing bowl, combine the olive oil, finely chopped chipotle peppers, minced garlic, lime zest, lime juice, ground cumin, smoked paprika, chili powder, salt, and black pepper. Mix well to make the marinade.
2. Add the peeled and deveined shrimp to the marinade, making sure they are evenly coated. Cover the bowl and let the shrimp marinate in the refrigerator for at least 30 minutes, or up to 2 hours.
3. Heat a large skillet over medium-high heat. Once hot, add the marinated shrimp in a single layer, making sure not to overcrowd the skillet. Cook the shrimp for 2-3 minutes on each side, or until they are pink and cooked through.
4. Once cooked, remove the shrimp from the skillet and transfer them to a serving plate.
5. Garnish the Spicy Chipotle Lime Shrimp with chopped fresh cilantro.
6. Serve the shrimp hot, with lime wedges on the side for squeezing.

Enjoy the bold and zesty flavors of this Spicy Chipotle Lime Shrimp as a delicious appetizer or main dish! Adjust the level of spiciness by adding more or less chipotle peppers according to your preference.

Spicy Korean Bulgogi

Ingredients:

- 1 lb (about 450g) thinly sliced beef (such as ribeye or sirloin)
- 1/4 cup soy sauce
- 2 tablespoons brown sugar
- 2 tablespoons sesame oil
- 3 cloves garlic, minced
- 1 tablespoon grated ginger
- 2 green onions, chopped
- 1 tablespoon gochujang (Korean red chili paste)
- 1 tablespoon gochugaru (Korean red chili flakes) (adjust to taste)
- 1 tablespoon rice vinegar
- 1 tablespoon honey
- 1 tablespoon toasted sesame seeds
- 2 tablespoons vegetable oil, for cooking
- Cooked rice, for serving
- Sliced green onions and toasted sesame seeds for garnish (optional)

Instructions:

1. In a mixing bowl, combine the soy sauce, brown sugar, sesame oil, minced garlic, grated ginger, chopped green onions, gochujang, gochugaru, rice vinegar, honey, and toasted sesame seeds. Mix well to make the marinade.
2. Add the thinly sliced beef to the marinade, making sure it is evenly coated. Cover the bowl and let it marinate in the refrigerator for at least 30 minutes, or up to 2 hours for maximum flavor.
3. Heat a large skillet or grill pan over medium-high heat. Add the vegetable oil to the skillet.
4. Once hot, add the marinated beef to the skillet in a single layer, making sure not to overcrowd the pan. Cook the beef for 2-3 minutes on each side, or until browned and cooked through.
5. Once cooked, remove the beef from the skillet and transfer it to a serving plate.
6. Serve the Spicy Korean Bulgogi hot, with steamed rice.
7. Garnish with sliced green onions and toasted sesame seeds, if desired.

Enjoy the flavorful and spicy Spicy Korean Bulgogi as a delicious and satisfying meal! Adjust the level of spiciness by adding more or less gochugaru according to your preference.

Spicy Szechuan Dan Dan Noodles

Ingredients:

For the Sauce:

- 3 tablespoons soy sauce
- 2 tablespoons Chinese black vinegar (or substitute with rice vinegar)
- 1 tablespoon sesame oil
- 1 tablespoon chili oil
- 2 teaspoons sugar
- 2 cloves garlic, minced
- 1 teaspoon grated ginger
- 1 tablespoon Szechuan peppercorns, toasted and ground
- 2 green onions, chopped (for garnish)
- 2 tablespoons chopped roasted peanuts (for garnish)

For the Noodles:

- 8 oz (about 225g) fresh or dried Chinese wheat noodles (such as egg noodles or udon noodles)
- 1/2 lb (about 225g) ground pork or chicken (optional)
- 2 tablespoons vegetable oil
- 2 cloves garlic, minced
- 1 tablespoon Szechuan chili bean paste (doubanjiang)
- 1 teaspoon Szechuan peppercorns, toasted and ground
- 2 cups chicken broth or water
- Salt to taste
- Chopped cilantro for garnish (optional)

Instructions:

1. Cook the noodles according to the package instructions until al dente. Drain and set aside.
2. In a small bowl, whisk together the soy sauce, Chinese black vinegar, sesame oil, chili oil, sugar, minced garlic, grated ginger, and ground Szechuan peppercorns to make the sauce. Set aside.

3. In a large skillet or wok, heat the vegetable oil over medium heat. Add the ground pork or chicken (if using) and cook until browned and cooked through. Remove from the skillet and set aside.
4. In the same skillet, add the minced garlic and cook for 1-2 minutes until fragrant.
5. Add the Szechuan chili bean paste (doubanjiang) and ground Szechuan peppercorns to the skillet. Stir-fry for another minute.
6. Return the cooked ground pork or chicken to the skillet. Stir to combine with the chili bean paste mixture.
7. Pour in the chicken broth or water and bring the mixture to a simmer.
8. Add the cooked noodles to the skillet. Toss everything together until the noodles are evenly coated with the sauce.
9. Season with salt to taste, if needed.
10. Divide the Spicy Szechuan Dan Dan Noodles among serving bowls.
11. Drizzle the prepared sauce over the noodles.
12. Garnish with chopped green onions, chopped roasted peanuts, and chopped cilantro, if desired.
13. Serve the noodles hot, and enjoy!

These Spicy Szechuan Dan Dan Noodles are bursting with flavor and perfect for spice lovers. Adjust the level of spiciness by adding more or less chili oil and Szechuan peppercorns according to your preference.

Spicy Mango Chicken Salad

Ingredients:

For the Salad:

- 2 boneless, skinless chicken breasts
- Salt and black pepper to taste
- 1 tablespoon olive oil
- 6 cups mixed salad greens (such as spinach, arugula, and romaine)
- 1 ripe mango, peeled, pitted, and diced
- 1/2 red bell pepper, diced
- 1/4 cup red onion, thinly sliced
- 1/4 cup chopped fresh cilantro
- 1/4 cup chopped roasted peanuts or cashews (optional)

For the Spicy Mango Dressing:

- 1 ripe mango, peeled, pitted, and diced
- 2 tablespoons lime juice
- 1 tablespoon honey or maple syrup
- 1 tablespoon rice vinegar
- 1 tablespoon soy sauce
- 1 teaspoon grated ginger
- 1/2 teaspoon chili flakes (adjust to taste)
- 2 tablespoons olive oil
- Salt and black pepper to taste

Instructions:

1. Season the chicken breasts with salt and black pepper on both sides.
2. Heat the olive oil in a skillet over medium-high heat. Add the seasoned chicken breasts to the skillet and cook for 5-6 minutes on each side, or until cooked through and no longer pink in the center. Remove from the skillet and let them rest for a few minutes before slicing.

3. In a large bowl, combine the mixed salad greens, diced mango, diced red bell pepper, thinly sliced red onion, and chopped fresh cilantro. Toss gently to combine.
4. In a blender or food processor, combine the diced mango, lime juice, honey or maple syrup, rice vinegar, soy sauce, grated ginger, chili flakes, olive oil, salt, and black pepper. Blend until smooth and creamy.
5. Slice the cooked chicken breasts into thin strips.
6. Add the sliced chicken to the salad bowl.
7. Drizzle the Spicy Mango Dressing over the salad and toss gently to coat everything evenly.
8. Divide the Spicy Mango Chicken Salad among serving plates.
9. Garnish with chopped roasted peanuts or cashews, if desired.
10. Serve the salad immediately and enjoy!

This Spicy Mango Chicken Salad is refreshing, flavorful, and packed with nutrients.

Adjust the level of spiciness by adding more or fewer chili flakes according to your preference.

Spicy Buffalo Cauliflower Pizza

Ingredients:

For the Buffalo Cauliflower:

- 1 medium head cauliflower, cut into florets
- 2 tablespoons olive oil
- Salt and black pepper to taste
- 1/2 cup buffalo sauce (such as Frank's RedHot)
- 2 tablespoons unsalted butter, melted
- 1 tablespoon honey or maple syrup (optional, for sweetness)
- 1 teaspoon garlic powder
- 1/2 teaspoon smoked paprika

For the Pizza:

- 1 pre-made pizza dough (store-bought or homemade)
- 1/2 cup buffalo sauce
- 1 cup shredded mozzarella cheese
- 1/4 cup crumbled blue cheese
- 2 green onions, thinly sliced
- Ranch or blue cheese dressing for drizzling (optional)
- Chopped fresh cilantro or parsley for garnish (optional)

Instructions:

1. Preheat your oven to 425°F (220°C). If using a pizza stone, place it in the oven to preheat as well.
2. In a large mixing bowl, toss the cauliflower florets with olive oil, salt, and black pepper until evenly coated.
3. Spread the cauliflower florets in a single layer on a baking sheet lined with parchment paper or aluminum foil.
4. Roast the cauliflower in the preheated oven for 20-25 minutes, or until golden brown and tender, flipping halfway through.
5. In a small bowl, whisk together the buffalo sauce, melted butter, honey or maple syrup (if using), garlic powder, and smoked paprika.
6. Once the cauliflower is roasted, transfer it to a large mixing bowl. Pour the buffalo sauce mixture over the cauliflower and toss until evenly coated.

7. Increase the oven temperature to 475°F (245°C).
8. Roll out the pizza dough on a lightly floured surface into your desired shape and thickness.
9. Transfer the rolled-out dough to a pizza stone or baking sheet lined with parchment paper.
10. Spread the remaining 1/2 cup of buffalo sauce evenly over the pizza dough.
11. Sprinkle the shredded mozzarella cheese over the buffalo sauce.
12. Arrange the buffalo cauliflower over the cheese.
13. Sprinkle the crumbled blue cheese over the top.
14. Bake the pizza in the preheated oven for 12-15 minutes, or until the crust is golden brown and the cheese is bubbly and melted.
15. Remove the pizza from the oven and let it cool for a few minutes.
16. Drizzle ranch or blue cheese dressing over the top, if desired.
17. Garnish with thinly sliced green onions and chopped fresh cilantro or parsley, if desired.
18. Slice the Spicy Buffalo Cauliflower Pizza and serve hot.

Enjoy the spicy and flavorful Spicy Buffalo Cauliflower Pizza as a delicious and satisfying meal! Adjust the level of spiciness by adding more or less buffalo sauce according to your preference.

Spicy Jalapeno Margarita

Ingredients:

- 2 oz (60 ml) silver tequila
- 1 oz (30 ml) triple sec or orange liqueur
- 1 oz (30 ml) freshly squeezed lime juice
- 1/2 oz (15 ml) agave syrup or simple syrup (adjust to taste)
- 1/4 to 1/2 jalapeno pepper, sliced (adjust to desired spice level)
- Ice cubes
- Salt or Tajin for rimming the glass (optional)
- Lime wedges for garnish

Instructions:

1. Rim the edge of a margarita glass with salt or Tajin, if desired. Rub a lime wedge around the rim of the glass, then dip it into a plate with salt or Tajin to coat the rim.
2. In a cocktail shaker, muddle the sliced jalapeno pepper to release its flavor and spice. If you prefer a spicier margarita, add more jalapeno slices.
3. Add tequila, triple sec or orange liqueur, lime juice, and agave syrup or simple syrup to the shaker.
4. Fill the shaker with ice cubes.
5. Close the shaker tightly and shake vigorously for about 10-15 seconds to chill the drink and incorporate all the ingredients.
6. Strain the margarita into the prepared glass filled with ice cubes.
7. Garnish with a lime wedge.
8. If desired, you can adjust the spice level by adding more jalapeno slices directly into the glass or by muddling them further.
9. Serve immediately and enjoy your Spicy Jalapeno Margarita!

Feel free to adjust the sweetness level by adding more or less agave syrup or simple syrup according to your preference. You can also customize the spice level by adding more or fewer jalapeno slices. Cheers!

Spicy Thai Red Curry

Ingredients:

- 2 tablespoons vegetable oil
- 2 tablespoons Thai red curry paste
- 1 can (14 oz) coconut milk
- 1 cup vegetable broth or chicken broth
- 1 tablespoon fish sauce (optional, omit for vegetarian/vegan)
- 1 tablespoon brown sugar or palm sugar
- 1 red bell pepper, sliced
- 1 green bell pepper, sliced
- 1 small eggplant, diced
- 1 cup sliced mushrooms (such as button mushrooms or shiitake mushrooms)
- 1 cup diced tofu, chicken, or shrimp (optional)
- 1 cup packed baby spinach leaves
- 1 tablespoon lime juice
- Fresh Thai basil leaves or cilantro for garnish
- Cooked rice, for serving

Instructions:

1. Heat the vegetable oil in a large skillet or wok over medium heat.
2. Add the Thai red curry paste to the skillet and stir-fry for 1-2 minutes until fragrant.
3. Pour in the coconut milk and vegetable broth or chicken broth, stirring to combine.
4. Stir in the fish sauce (if using) and brown sugar. Bring the mixture to a simmer.
5. Add the sliced red bell pepper, green bell pepper, diced eggplant, sliced mushrooms, and diced tofu, chicken, or shrimp (if using) to the skillet. Stir to combine.
6. Simmer the curry for 8-10 minutes, or until the vegetables are tender and the sauce has thickened slightly.
7. Stir in the baby spinach leaves and lime juice. Cook for another 1-2 minutes until the spinach wilts.
8. Taste the curry and adjust the seasoning if needed, adding more fish sauce or lime juice to balance the flavors.
9. Remove the skillet from heat.
10. Serve the Spicy Thai Red Curry hot over cooked rice.

11. Garnish with fresh Thai basil leaves or cilantro.

Enjoy the flavorful and spicy Spicy Thai Red Curry as a delicious and comforting meal! Adjust the level of spiciness by adding more or less Thai red curry paste according to your preference.

Spicy Cajun Shrimp Po' Boy

Ingredients:

For the Cajun Shrimp:

- 1 lb (about 450g) large shrimp, peeled and deveined
- 2 tablespoons Cajun seasoning
- 2 tablespoons olive oil
- Salt and black pepper to taste

For the Remoulade Sauce:

- 1/2 cup mayonnaise
- 2 tablespoons Dijon mustard
- 1 tablespoon hot sauce (such as Tabasco)
- 1 tablespoon Worcestershire sauce
- 1 tablespoon chopped fresh parsley
- 1 clove garlic, minced
- Salt and black pepper to taste

For Assembling the Po' Boy:

- 4-6 soft French baguettes or sub rolls, split lengthwise
- 2 cups shredded lettuce
- 1 large tomato, thinly sliced
- Sliced pickles (optional)
- Sliced red onion (optional)
- Sliced jalapenos (optional)

Instructions:

1. Preheat the oven to 375°F (190°C).
2. In a large bowl, toss the peeled and deveined shrimp with Cajun seasoning, olive oil, salt, and black pepper until evenly coated.

3. Heat a skillet or grill pan over medium-high heat. Once hot, add the seasoned shrimp to the skillet in a single layer. Cook for 2-3 minutes on each side, or until the shrimp are pink and cooked through. Remove from heat.
4. While the shrimp are cooking, prepare the remoulade sauce. In a small bowl, whisk together the mayonnaise, Dijon mustard, hot sauce, Worcestershire sauce, chopped parsley, minced garlic, salt, and black pepper until smooth. Adjust the seasoning to taste.
5. Place the split French baguettes or sub rolls on a baking sheet. Toast them in the preheated oven for 3-5 minutes, or until lightly golden and crispy.
6. To assemble the Po' Boys, spread a generous amount of remoulade sauce on the toasted baguettes or sub rolls.
7. Arrange shredded lettuce on one side of the bread, followed by sliced tomatoes.
8. Place the cooked Cajun shrimp on top of the tomatoes.
9. Add any optional toppings such as sliced pickles, red onion, or jalapenos, if desired.
10. Close the Po' Boys and press down gently to flatten slightly.
11. Serve the Spicy Cajun Shrimp Po' Boys immediately, and enjoy!

These Spicy Cajun Shrimp Po' Boys are bursting with flavor and perfect for a satisfying meal. Adjust the level of spiciness by adding more or less Cajun seasoning according to your preference.

www.ingramcontent.com/pod-product-compliance
Lightning Source LLC
LaVergne TN
LVHW061945070526
838199LV00060B/3980